ELEMENTS OF FICTION

Elements of Fiction

ROBERT SCHOLES

New York
OXFORD UNIVERSITY PRESS
London   Toronto   1968

For William M. Sale, Jr.

ON THE ELEMENTARINESS OF THIS TEXT

This book is elementary in two somewhat different senses. First, it is aimed at the beginner in the study of fiction, not at the expert. Second, it attempts to deal with fundamentals rather than with refinements. It does not offer complicated systems of classification or an elaborate critical vocabulary, but it does present some basic conceptual tools for the analysis and interpretation of fiction. In writing the pages that follow, I have tried to be plain and straightforward without oversimplifying the complicated realities (and unrealities) of fiction. And I have tried to confine my remarks as much as possible to practical suggestions about the reading process. A book like this should maintain resolutely its "secondary" status. It is not an object to be studied for its own sake but an implement designed to assist the reader in dealing with "primary" materials —works of fiction themselves.

CONTENTS

shape. Plain enough words, one would think—not necessarily loaded with overtones of approval or disapproval. But their fortunes in the world of words have not been equal. Fact has prospered. In our ordinary conversation "fact" is associated with those pillars of verbal society, "reality" and "truth." "Fiction," on the other hand, is known to consort with such suspicious characters as "unreality" and "falsehood." Still, if we look into the matter, we can see that the relationship of "fact" and "fiction" with "the real" and "the true" is not exactly what appears on the surface. Fact still means for us quite literally "a thing done." And fiction has never lost its meaning of "a thing made." But in what sense do things done or things made partake of truth or reality? A thing done has no real existence once it has been done. It may have consequences, and there may be many records that point to its former existence (think of the Civil War, for example), but once it is done its existence is finished. A thing made, on the other hand, exists until it decays or is destroyed. Once it is finished its existence begins (think of a Civil War story like Crane's *Red Badge of Courage*, for example). Fact finally has no real existence, while fiction may last for centuries.

We can see this rather strange relation between fact and fiction more clearly if we consider one place where the two come together: the place we call history. The word "history" itself hides a double meaning. It comes from a Greek word which originally meant inquiry or investigation. But it soon acquired the two meanings which interest us here: on the one hand history can mean "things that have happened"; on the other it can refer to "a recorded version of things that are supposed to have happened." That is, history can mean both the events of the past and the story of these events: fact—or fiction. The very word "story" lurks in the word "history," and is derived from it. What begins as investigation must end as story. Fact, in order to survive, must become fiction. Seen in this way, fiction is not the opposite of fact, but its complement. It gives a more lasting shape to the vanishing deeds of men.

But this is, in fact, only one aspect of fiction. We *do* think of it also as something quite different from historical records or mere data. We think of it not just as made but as made-up, a non-natural, unreal product of the human imagination. It is helpful to see fiction in both of the ways outlined here. It can be very factual, maintaining the closest possible correspondence between its story and things that have actually happened in the world. Or it can be very fanciful, defying our sense of life's ordinary possibilities. Taking these two extremes as the opposite ends of a whole spectrum of fictional possibilities, between the infra-red of pure history and the ultra-violet of pure imagination we can distinguish many shades of coloration. But all are fragments of the white radiance of truth, which is present in both history books and fairy tales, but only partly present in each—fragmented by the prism of fiction, without which we should not be able to see it at all. For truth is like ordinary light, present everywhere but invisible, and we must break it to behold it. To fracture truth in a purposeful and pleasing way—that is the job of the writer of fiction, with whatever shades from the spectrum he chooses to work.

II FICTION: EXPERIENCE AND ANALYSIS

Though fiction itself has a real existence—a book has weight and occupies space—our experience of fiction is unreal. When we are reading a story we are not "doing" anything. We have stopped the ordinary course of our existence, severed our connections with friends and family, in order to withdraw temporarily into a private and unreal world. Our experience of fiction is more like dreaming than like our normal waking activity. It makes us physically inert but exercises our imagination. In terms of our performing any action in it, this special world is absolutely unreal, whether we are reading a history book or a science fiction story. We can do nothing to affect either the Battle of Waterloo or the War of the Worlds. And yet, in a way, we participate. We are engaged and involved in the events we are reading about, though powerless to alter them. We *experience* the events of a story, but without the consequences—emerging from John Hersey's *Hiro-*

shima without a scratch on our bodies. Emotionally, however, and intellectually, we are different. We have experienced something.

All discussion of literature, all classes and instruction in literary matters, can have only one valid end: to prepare us for our part in the literary experience. Just as the dull routine exercises and repetitious practice for an athletic event or a dramatic performance are devoted to the end of physical and mental readiness for the actual game or play, exercises in literature are preparations for the act of reading. The successful athlete must do much "instinctively," moving faster than thought to make the most of his time. The painstaking analysis of "game movies" by football coach and players, the searching criticism of each player's reactions to every situation, the drill to counteract past errors—all these wait upon the test of the game itself. Then ability, experience, and training will reveal their quality. It is similar with reading. Classroom, teacher, the artificially assembled anthology—all these must give place to that final confrontation between individual reader and story. Only this is not a struggle like an athletic contest, but something more intimate and more rewarding. Ideally, it is a kind of consummation —an embrace.

Everything that follows in this book is intended to help readers toward an enriched experience of fiction. Such special terminology as is presented is presented not because critical terminology is an important object of study. Its acquisition is not an end in itself. We learn terminology in order to analyze more accurately. We learn the process of analysis in order to read better. Period.

III   THE SPECTRUM OF FICTION

The fictional spectrum mentioned earlier can be of use in the analysis of fiction, so long as we remember that it is just a metaphor, a handy linguistic tool to be discarded when it becomes more of a hindrance to understanding than a help. In terms of this metaphor, you will remember, it was possible to think of fiction as resembling the spectrum of color to be found in ordinary light, but in the fictional spectrum the ends were not infra-red and ultra-violet but history and fantasy.

Now only a recording angel, taking note of all the deeds of men without distorting or omitting anything, could be called a "pure" historian. And only a kind of deity, creating a world out of his own imagination, could be called a "pure" fantasist. Both ends of the spectrum are invisible to mortal eyes. All history recorded by men becomes fictional. All human fantasy involves some resemblance—however far-fetched—to life. For the student of fiction, then, the *combination* of historical and imaginative materials becomes crucial. This is so because our understanding of fiction depends on our grasping the way in which any particular work is related to life.

Life itself is neither tragic nor comic, neither sentimental nor ironic. It is a sequence of sensations, actions, thoughts, and events which we try to tame with language. Every time we say a word about our existence we are engaged in this taming process. An art like fiction is a very highly developed method of domestication, in which life is not merely subdued but is asked to perform tricks as well. The tricks, if well done, please us in a very complicated way. In the first place they please because their order and intelligibility are a welcome relief from the confusions and pressures of daily existence. And in the second place this artificial order can be mastered by us and used to help make sense of our own experience. Having read Hemingway or Conrad, we will begin to recognize certain situations in our existence as having a family resemblance to situations we have encountered in the pages of Conrad or Hemingway. Literature offers us an "escape" out of life, but also provides us with new equipment for our inevitable return. It offers us an "imitation" of life. It helps us understand life and life helps us understand fiction. We recognize aspects of ourselves and our situations in the more ordered perspectives of fiction, and we also see ideal and debased extremes of existence—both possible and impossible—which are interesting in themselves and interestingly different from our own experience. Fiction interests us because of the complicated ways in which it is at once like and unlike life, which is what we mean when we say it is an "imitation." Our experience of fiction, then, involves both pleasure and understanding. We can think of understanding either as a result of the pleasurable experience of fiction or as a necessary preliminary to that pleasure. But no matter how we view the complicated relationship between pleasure and understanding, we must recognize that the two are inseparable in the reading of fiction.

Now it happens that education has more to do with understanding than with pleasure. This is regrettable, perhaps, but unavoidable. In our study of fiction, then, we must concentrate on understanding and hope that pleasure will follow because of the connection between the two. Understanding a work of fiction begins with recognizing what kind of fiction it is. This is where the notion of a spectrum becomes useful. We can adjust to the special qualities of any given work more readily if we begin it with a clear and flexible view of fictional possibilities.

Any attempt to give every shade of fiction a place would be cumbersome and misleading. What we want is a rough scale only, with the primary possibilities noted and located in relation to one another. Between the extremes of history and fantasy on such a scale we might locate two major points of reference something like this:

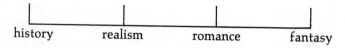

"Realism" and "romance" are names of the two principal ways fiction can be related to life. Realism is a matter of perception. The realist presents his impressions of the world of experience. Some of his vocabulary and other technical instruments he shares with the social scientists—especially the psychologists and sociologists. The realistic writer seeks always to give the reader a sense of the way things are, but he feels that a made-up structure of character and event can do better justice to the way things are than any attempt to copy reality directly. The realist's truth is a bit more general and typical than the reporter's fact. It may also be more vivid and memorable.

Romance is a matter of vision. The romancer presents not so much his impressions of the world as his ideas about it. The ordinary world is seen at a greater distance, and its shape and color are deliberately altered by the lenses and filters of philosophy and fantasy. In the world of romance, ideas are allowed to play less encumbered by data. Yet though "what is" often gives way in romance to "what ought to be" or "might be," ought and might always imply what is by their distortion of it.

Realism and romance are not absolutely different. They share some qualities between them. Realism itself is more romantic than history or journalism. (It is not reality, after all, but real*ism*.) And romance is more realistic than fantasy. Many important works of fiction are rich and complicated blends of romance and realism. In fact, it is possible to say that the greatest works are those which succeed in blending the realist's perception and the romancer's vision, giving us fictional worlds remarkably close to our sense of the actual, but skillfully shaped so as to make us intensely aware of the meaningful potential of existence.

IV   FICTIONAL MODES AND PATTERNS

The usefulness of the concept of a fictional spectrum will depend upon our ability to adapt it to various works of fiction. Such adaptation will inevitably require a certain amount of complication. The additional concepts of fictional modes and patterns will be a step in that direction. The spectrum assumed that romance diverges from realism in one way only, along that line which leads from history to fantasy. But it is possible to see this divergence in a more complete way by observing that there are actually two quite different modes of what we have been calling romance.

We can begin by noting that there are two obvious ways that reality can be distorted by fiction. It can be made to appear better or worse than we actually believe it to be. These distortions are ways of seeing certain aspects of reality more clearly at the expense of others. They can present a "true" picture of either the heroic or the debased side of human existence. A fictional work which presents a world better than the real world is in the mode of romance. A work which presents a fictional world worse than the real world is in the mode of anti-romance, or satire. Because they represent certain potentialities that we recognize as present in our world, both these distorted views depend on our sense of the actual to make their effects.

The world of romance emphasizes beauty and order. The world of satire emphasizes ugliness and disorder. The relationships between individual characters and these distorted worlds constitute a crucial element of fiction, for these relationships determine certain patterns or master plots which affect the shaping of the particular plot of every story. One of these master patterns deals with the kind of character who begins out of harmony with his world and is gradually educated or initiated into a harmonious situation in it. This pattern can operate in either the ordered world of romance or the chaotic world of satire, but the same pattern will have a quite different effect on us when we observe it working out in such different situations. Education which adapts the inept or foolish character for a role in the orderly world presents a comic rise which we observe with approval and pleasure. An initiation into a world of ugliness and disorder, however, amounts to corruption, an ironic rise to what Milton called a "bad eminence," and we react with disapproval and disgust. (For some reason we find both reactions pleasurable.)

Another master pattern reverses this process of accommodation and presents us with change of another sort: the character who begins in harmony with his world but is finally rejected or destroyed by it. Again, depending on our view of the world presented, we react differently. The heroic figure who falls from his position in the orderly world through some flaw in his character is tragic. The lowly creature whose doom is the result of his unfortunate virtue or delicacy is pathetic. His fall is, ironically, a kind of rise. (It is traditionally assumed, for complicated reasons, that tragedy is superior to pathos. That assumption is not made here. These patterns are presented as descriptions only, not evaluations.)

The comic rise and the tragic fall are straightforward because the values of the orderly world represent human virtue raised to a heroic power. The satiric rise and pathetic fall are ironic because of the inverted values of the debased world. Satire and pathos debase the world in order to criticize it. Tragedy and comedy elevate it to make it acceptable. The two romantic patterns promote resignation. The two satiric patterns foment opposition.

One other pair of fictional patterns can be added to the two already considered. When characters begin and end in a harmonious relationship to their worlds, the fictional pattern is one not of change but of movement. The characters will have adventures or encounters but will not make any fundamental change in themselves or their relationship to the world around them. In this kind of story the hero himself will not be as important as the things he meets. In the romantic world the adventures of the hero will take the form of a quest or voyage which ends with his triumphant return and/or his marriage to the heroine. This pattern moves us to admiration of the wonderful, offering us more of an escape from the actual than a criticism of it. In the satiric world the adventures of a born anti-hero or rogue will parody the quest pattern, often reflecting the chaos of the debased world by becoming endless themselves. Stories of this kind are likely to end with the rogue heading for new territory or another tour of the familiar chaos. This picaresque pattern moves us to a recognition of the chaotic and toward an acceptance of it.

Thus we have distinguished three pairs of fictional patterns, or six kinds in all: the comic and the satiric rise; the tragic and the pathetic fall; the heroic (romantic) and the anti-heroic (picaresque) quest. But we have done this only with regard to the fantasy worlds of romance and satire, leaving open the question of what happens as these patterns are introduced into a more realistic fictional universe. What happens is, naturally, very complicated indeed. These neat, schematic distinctions fade; the various patterns combine and interact; and values themselves are called into question: rise and fall, success and failure—all become problematic. And this problematic quality is one of the great sources of interest in realistic fiction. Realism uses the familiar patterns of education, expulsion, and quest, but often in such a way as to call into question the great issues of whether the education is beneficial, the expulsion or death justified, the quest worthwhile. Our recognition of the traces of traditional patterns in realistic fiction will be of use, then, mainly in helping us to see what questions are being raised.

Historically, realism developed later than romance and satire; thus it will be useful for us to see realistic fiction as combining the elements of its predecessors in various ways. It would be a mistake, however, to think of realism as superseding the earlier forms just because it uses some of their elements in a new way. In fact, the development of realism has led to a kind of counterflow of realistic elements into the older forms of fiction, reinvigorating them with its problematical qualities. The reader of contemporary fiction in particular will require that flexibility of response which can be attained by careful attention to the workings of traditional patterns in modern fiction. But our discernment of these patterns in any work of fiction will depend on our grasp of the specific elements of that work. We must be alert to the way that *its* characters, *its* plot, and *its* point of view adapt the traditional elements we have been considering.

V PLOT

Fiction is movement. A story is a story because it tells
about a process of change. A man's situation changes.
Or he himself is changed in some way. Or our understanding of him changes. These are the essential movements of fiction. Learning to read stories involves
learning to "see" these movements, to follow them,
and to interpret them. In the classroom we often—
perhaps too often—put our emphasis on interpretation.
But you cannot interpret what you cannot see. Thus,
before getting into more complicated questions of interpretation, I want to give the plainest and most direct advice possible about how to perceive and follow
fictional plotting. This advice includes things to be
done while reading and things to be done after a first
reading. A good story can be experienced pleasurably
many times, and often a second or third reading will
be better in every respect than the first time through.

1. *Look at beginnings and endings.* Movement in fiction is always movement *from* and *to*. A grasp of the
start and the finish should lead to a sense of the direction taken to get *from* start to finish.

2. *Isolate the central characters.* The things that happen in fiction happen *to* somebody. A few major characters or even a single central character may be the
real focus of our concern. Explore the situation of the

major characters (or central character) at the beginning and the end of the story. The nature of the changes revealed by this exploration should begin to suggest what the story is all about.

3. *Note the stages in all important changes.* If a character has moved from one situation to another, or one state of mind to another, the steps leading to the completed change should be illuminating. Through them the reader can get to "how" and "why." But, as always, "what" comes first.

4. *Note the things working against the movement of the story.* Usually, the interest of a story can be seen as the product of two forces, those things which work to move it toward its end, and those things which work against that movement, delaying its completion. If the story moves toward a marriage, for example, consider what things delay the happy occasion. When we see the obstacles clearly, we should have a better sense of the direction of the plot itself.

5. *In a long story or novel consider the various lines of action.* A complex fiction is likely to involve a number of actions, each with its own central character. The actions may or may not interact. The central character in one line of action may be insignificant in another. By isolating the various lines of action and separating them from one another in our thoughts, we should gain a better sense of those things that connect

movement of fiction and to lead him toward an interest in character for its own sake. Using the newly developed ideas we have learned to call psychology and sociology, the realistic writers have offered us instruction in human nature. The motivation of characters, the workings of conscience and consciousness, have been made the focal point of most novels and short stories. Perhaps the most extreme movement in this direction has been the development of the stream of consciousness technique, through which writers offer us a version of mental process at the level where impressions of things seen and heard converge with confused thoughts and longings arising from the subconscious mind. In reading this kind of fiction we must check the validity of its characterization against our own sense of the way people behave. The best realists always offer us a shock of recognition through which we share their perception of human behavior.

But earlier writers of fiction and many contemporary writers have not made the realistic presentation of character their main interest. For some, the telling of an exciting story is an end in itself. They do not shy away from improbable or even fantastic events. The characters in non-realistic tales and romances are likely to be sketched in rather than presented in depth; and they will tend toward extremes of beauty and ugliness, goodness and badness. Some writers of fiction fill out the thinness of such characters—not with the psychological details of realism—but with ideas and attitudes drawn from philosophy and theology. Such writing is allegorical. It offers a meaning beyond the apparent significance of the story itself. Allegory was the most important form of fiction in the Middle Ages and is now becoming important again, as writers like John Barth, William Golding, and Iris Murdoch draw upon philosophy in their characterization and plotting. A little reading in the Existentialist philosophers can be a big help in understanding certain kinds of contemporary fiction.

It may be useful for us to think of character as a function of two impulses: the impulse to individualize and the impulse to typify. Great and memorable characters are the result of a powerful combination of these two impulses. We remember the special, individualizing quirks—habitual patterns of speech, action, or appearance—and we remember the way the character represents something larger than himself. These individualizing touches are part of the story-teller's art. They amuse us or engage our sympathy for the character. The typifying touches are part of a story's meaning. In realistic fiction a character is likely to be representative of a social class, a race, a profession; or he may be a recognizable psychological type, analyzable in terms of this or that "complex" or "syndrome." Or he may be a mixture of social and psychological qualities. In allegorical fiction the characters are more likely to represent philosophical positions. In a story of adventure we will encounter types belonging to the traditional pattern of romantic quest: hero, heroine, villain, monster.

The important thing for a reader to remember about characterization is that there are many varieties of it—and many combinations of the varieties. An adventure story can have an important realistic or allegorical dimension which will be observable in its characterizations. Characters in realistic novels may also be meaningful as illustrations of philosophical ideas or attitudes. As readers we must be alert and ready to respond to different kinds of characterization in their own terms. A story by J. L. Borges and a story by James Joyce are not likely to yield equally to the same kind of reading. It is the reader's business to adapt himself to whatever fictional world he enters. It is the writer's business to make such adaptation worthwhile.

VII   MEANING

More often than not, when we talk about a story after our experience of it, we talk about its meaning. In the classroom, "What is the theme of this work?" is a favorite question. This interpretive aspect of literary analysis is the most difficult, I should say, because in order to attempt it we must not only look carefully at the work itself but also look away from the work toward the world of ideas and experiences. Discovering themes or meanings in a work involves us in making

connections between the work and the world outside
it. These connections *are* the meaning. The great problem for the interpreter, then, becomes that of the validity of the thematic materials he discovers. Are these
ideas *really* there? we want to know. Are they being
"read out" of the story or "read into" it? Is any given
set of connections between story and world necessarily
implied by the story itself or are they arbitrarily im-
posed by an overly clever interpreter?

A story is always particular, always an instance.
How do we properly move from any given instance to
a general notion? When is it legitimate to conclude
from the presence of a husband and wife in a story
(for example) that the story is "about" marriage—that
it makes a statement or raises a question about this
aspect of human relationships? It is impossible to provide a single method that will always work. In fact,
as T. S. Eliot once observed, "There is no method ex-
cept to be very intelligent." But there are certain procedures that will frequently prove helpful, even for the
very intelligent.

If we isolate everything in a story which is not just
narration, description, or dialogue, some clues are
likely to appear. The title of a work is often a striking
instance of this kind of material. Sometimes it will
point our thinking about the work in a particular
direction, or it will emphasize for us the importance
of a particular element in the work. Like the title,
passages in the story which are themselves com-

mentary or interpretation are of especial importance for thematic discussion. Often, however, interpretive passages will not be presented directly by a narrator, with all his authority behind them. They will be spoken instead by a character, which means that we must assess the reliability of the character before we decide to accept his interpretation as valid. Sometimes the narrator will be characterized to the extent that we must question even his reliability. In similar ways narration and description may also be colored by thematic materials. A character or a scene may be presented by the author so as to lead us toward a certain way of thinking about the materials presented. A school called "Dotheboys Hall" or a teacher named "Gradgrind" is presented to us with a name that carries some not too subtle advice as to how we are to understand the presentation.

In less obvious cases, where the author refrains from direct commentary, we must look for subtler clues. Patterns of repetition, ironic juxtapositions, the tone of the narration—things like these must lead us to the connections between the particular world of the book and the generalized world of ideas. And the more delicate and subtle the story is, the more delicate our interpretation must be. Thus, taking care that our interpretation is rooted in the work itself is only one aspect of the problem. The other aspect involves the outside knowledge that the interpreter brings to the work. If the story is realistic it will be understood best by those readers whose experience has equipped them with information about the aspect of reality toward which the story points. This does not mean that one must have been in an infantry battle to understand *The Red Badge of Courage*. But that novel does depend on the reader's having some understanding of fear and some sense of the way individuals are subjected to an intense social pressure to act with the opposite of fear—courage. Often a realistic novel may point to an aspect of life we have encountered but never understood, and the fiction may help us clarify and order that experience. D. H. Lawrence's *Sons and Lovers* can teach us something about the nature of personal relationships, especially about the way a mother's possessive love can cripple a young man emotionally and inhibit his growth as a man. But Lawrence requires us to bring some experience of family life and the emotional life to that novel, without which it must remain virtually meaningless for the reader. Fantasy and adventure are the main ingredients of the child's literary diet because the child lacks the experience that would make realism meaningful to him, and he lacks the learning which is necessary for the interpretation of allegorical fiction.

Often, however, allegorical fiction takes the form of fantasy or adventure so that it can be read by the child "on one level" and by the adult on two. *The Lord of the Flies* is a story of adventure. But it is also an allegory in which Reason and Gentleness struggle with

Fanaticism and Brutality. The free leader (Ralph), the inquiring rationalist (Piggy), and the dreaming vision- ary (Simon), are presented in that powerful tale as be- sieged by a bestiality which is also a part of man's nature. William Golding uses boys to represent these different potentialities in humanity, and he pessimisti- cally suggests that the evil in human nature is likely to get the better of the good. To read the novel in this way we need at least some skill in dealing with ab- stractions like good and evil, science and art, reason and instinct. And we need to follow the clues in the title and in the chapter called "Gift for the Darkness" in which Simon is spoken to by "the Lord of the Flies." If we see both the physical adventure and the adven- ture of ideas in the novel, we read with a double ex- citement. Of course, some works, like *Treasure Island*, offer us story for its own sake, in a pattern designed to offer us emotional stimulation without intellectual con- tent.

Fiction generates its meanings in innumerable ways, but always in terms of some movement from the par- ticular characters and events of the story to general ideas or human situations suggested by them. The reader comes to an understanding of a fictional work by locating the relevant generalities outside the work and fitting them to the specific instances within the work. The process of understanding can be crudely represented as a sequence something like this:

(a) The reader determines whether the work points mainly toward experience itself (i.e., is "realistic"), or toward ideas about experience (i.e., is "allegorical"), or is self-contained.

(b) Using the clues in the work he sifts his store of general notions drawn from experience or systematic thought to find those appropriate to the specific materials of the story.

(c) He checks back against the story to test the relevance of the general notions summoned up.

(d) He seeks for the way the story refines, qualifies, questions, or reinforces those notions.

Something like the process described—performed not a single time but in rapid oscillation into the work and back out—should leave the reader with an understanding of the story and with an enriched store of general notions which he has been led to develop in order to understand. In addition to acquiring new notions, he may have refined his attitudes toward his old notions and toward experience itself. Fiction is not justified as a means of conveying ideas but as a means of generating attitudes toward ideas. The meaning of fiction must finally be seen in terms of emotions directed toward impressions of experience or toward ideas about life.

VIII   POINT OF VIEW: PERSPECTIVE AND LANGUAGE

Point of view is a technical term for the way a story
is told. A stage play normally has no particular point
of view: no one stands between the audience and the
action. But if we *read* a play, the stage directions—the
words of someone who is not a character—provide
the beginnings of a special point of view. A story told all
in dialogue would be similarly without a point of view.
But as soon as a descriptive phrase is added—such as
"he said *cruelly*" or "she *whined viciously*"—we begin
to have a special viewpoint. A voice outside the action
is reaching us, shaping our attitude toward the events
being presented. In our experience of fiction, the attitude we develop toward the events presented, and our
understanding of those events, will usually be controlled by the author through his technical manage-
ment of point of view. For convenience we can divide
the subject of fictional viewpoint into two related parts
—one dealing with the nature of the story-teller in
any given fiction, and the other dealing with his language. Obviously the two are not really separate. Certain kinds of narration require certain kinds of language—Huck Finn must talk like Huck Finn—but we
can consider them apart for analytical purposes.

The nature of the story-teller is itself far from a
simple matter. It involves such things as the extent to

which he is himself a character whose personality affects our understanding of his statements, and the extent to which his view of events is limited in time and space or in his ability to see into the minds of various characters. The complications and refinements in fictional point of view can be classified at considerable length. But for the reader the classifications themselves are less important than his awareness of many possibilities. The reader's problem comes down to knowing how to take the things presented to him. This means paying special attention to any limitations in the narrator's viewpoint. If the viewpoint in the story is "partial"—in the sense of incomplete or in the sense of biased—the reader must be ready to compensate in appropriate ways.

The language of narration presents a similar problem for the reader—that is, a problem of adjustment and compensation. Of all the dimensions of language that can be considered, two are especially important for the reader of fiction. Both of these dimensions can be seen as ways in which wit—or artistic intelligence —operates through language. One has to do with tone, or the way unstated attitudes are conveyed through language. The other has to do with metaphor, or the way language can convey the richest and most delicate kinds of understanding by bringing together different images and ideas. Consider first this small passage from Virginia Woolf's novel *Mrs. Dalloway:*

> But Sir William Bradshaw stopped at the door
> to look at a picture. He looked in the corner for
> the engraver's name. His wife looked too. Sir
> William Bradshaw was so interested in art.

What is the tone of this? Sarcastic, I should say. The
paragraph asks us to be critical of the Bradshaws, but
it does not do so directly. It uses the indirection of
verbal irony in which the real meaning is different from
the apparent sense of the words. The last sentence might
be read aloud with a drawn-out emphasis on the word
"soooo." How do we know this? How do we supply
the appropriate tone of voice for words that we see on
the page but do not hear pronounced? We pay attention to the clues given. In *Mrs. Dalloway* the Bradshaws appear in a similar light several times; so that by
this, their last appearance, we have been prepared to
regard them unsympathetically. But just on the strength
of these four sentences we should be able to catch the
tone. The banal "Dick and Jane" sentence patterns
reinforce the banality of an approach to art by way of
the artist's name. Sir William looks not at the picture
itself but at the signature. The implication of this action
is that (a) he cannot tell who the artist is by considering the work alone, and (b) he attaches too much importance to the name. His interest in art is fraudulent.
Thus the statement that he is "so" interested in art
conflicts with both the actions narrated and the tone
of the narration. We resolve the conflict by reading the
sentence as ironic, meaning the opposite of what it

seems to say, and acquiring thereby a sarcastic tone. The way his wife's behavior mechanically mimics his own adds another satiric dimension to the little scene.

As an earlier passage in the noval has revealed to us, she has no life of her own but has been reduced by him to the status of an object:

> Fifteen years ago she had gone under. It was nothing you could put your finger on; there had been no scene, no snap; only the slow sinking, waterlogged, of her will into his.

Thus the short sentence—"His wife looked too"—picks up the earlier statement about the "submersion" of her will in his, and reminds us of it with satiric brevity. Catching the tone of a passage is a matter of paying attention to clues in sentence pattern and choice of words, and also of keeping in mind the whole context of the story we are reading. The more we read a particular author, the better we become at catching his tone—at perceiving the emotional shades that color the sense of his words.

The second passage I quoted from *Mrs. Dalloway* (which comes first in the book) is also a good introductory example of a writer's use of metaphor. The expression "gone under" has been used often enough to refer to defeat or failure—so often, in fact, that it is quite possible to use it without any sense that it is metaphorical. But actually the notion of drowning—going under water to the point of death—is present in the expression. A writer who, like Virginia Woolf, is sensitive to metaphor, can pick up the submerged (!) implications of such an expression and use them to strengthen her meaning: "the slow sinking, water-logged, of her will into his." The metaphor—which implicitly compares her to a floating object and him to the engulfing waters—conveys a sense of how slowly and inexorably this process has taken place, and it generates in us an appropriate feeling of horror at a human being's lingering destruction.

Similar metaphors can be used in different ways. In another part of the same novel Virginia Woolf employs the metaphor of drowning in a related but distinct context. When Peter Walsh, who wanted to marry Clarissa Dalloway in his youth, returns from India to tell her that he is in love with a young woman whom he intends to marry, Mrs. Dalloway reacts in this way:

> "In love!" she said. That he at his age should be sucked under in his little bow-tie by that monster! And there's no flesh on his neck; his hands are red; and he's six months older than I am! her eye flashed back to her; but in her heart she felt, all the same, he is in love. He has that, she felt; he is in love.

Love is seen here as a monstrous whirlpool which sucks people under. It is dangerous and destructive: one loses one's identity when sucked in by that monster. But it is also heroic to be involved in such dangerous matters. While her "eye" tells Mrs. Dalloway that Peter is unheroic and even ridiculous, with his little bow tie and skinny neck, her "heart" accepts the heroism of this venture. It is absurd to "be sucked under" in a "little bow tie," but it is also intensely real: "He has that, she felt; he is in love." By comparing these two metaphors of drowning we can see more accurately certain dimensions of Virginia Woolf's view of marriage: it involves a submergence or submission, but a violent conquest by an emotional whirlpool is superior to a "slow sinking, water-logged," of one will into another. We need not go outside the novel to understand this discrimination, but when we learn or remember that in a state of depression Mrs. Woolf took her own life by drowning, we get a hint of why this metaphor has such intensity in her hands.

These uses of the metaphor of drowning are actually just brief examples of the way metaphorical possibilities can be exploited in the language of fiction. I should like to present now a fuller example of metaphorical development, which the student can explore for himself. Marcel Proust's great multi-volume novel, *The Remembrance of Things Past*, is constructed around the recovery of the past in the memory of the central character and narrator, "Marcel." The process of recollection is described in a famous passage in which, on being given a piece of cake ("madeleine") dipped in tea, Marcel suddenly finds that the taste of this morsel of food has brought to mind much that he had forgotten. In the part of this passage quoted here, Marcel first discusses the persistence of sensations of taste and smell, and then considers the manner in which recollection can emerge from these sensations. The passage should be read with an eye to the metaphors (including similes) which operate in it:

> But when from a long-distant past nothing sub-sists, after the people are dead, after the things are broken and scattered, still, alone, more fragile, but with more vitality, more unsubstantial, more persistent, more faithful, the smell and taste of things remain poised a long time, like souls, ready to remind us, waiting and hoping for their moment, amid the ruins of all the rest; and bear unfalter-ing, in the tiny and almost impalpable drop of their essence, the vast structure of recollection.

> And once I had recognised the taste of the crumb of madeleine soaked in her decoction of lime-flowers which my aunt used to give me (al-though I did not yet know and must long postpone the discovery of why this memory made me so happy) immediately the old grey house upon the street, where her room was, rose up like the sce-nery of a theatre, to attach itself to the little pavil-ion, opening on to the garden, which had been built out behind it for my parents (the isolated panel which until that moment had been all that I could see); and with the house the town, from morning to night and in all weathers, the Square where I was sent before luncheon, the streets

along which I used to run errands, the country roads we took when it was fine. And just as the Japanese amuse themselves by filling a porcelain bowl with water and steeping in it little crumbs of paper which until then are without character or form, but, the moment they become wet, stretch themselves and bend, take on colour and distinctive shape, become flowers or houses or people, permanent and recognisable, so in that moment all the flowers in our garden and in M. Swann's park, and the water-lilies on the Vivonne and the good folk of the village and their little dwellings and the parish church and the whole of Combray and of its surroundings, taking their proper shapes and growing solid, sprang into being, town and gardens alike, from my cup of tea.

It is not my intention to encroach too much on what I feel should be matter for the student's consideration and discussion. But I wish to point out two of the principal metaphors in the passage and to make a suggestion or two about them. The first is the comparison of the smell and taste of things to "souls" in whose "essence" a shape or structure is housed. Proust is here using an ancient Greek notion of the soul as an essence which gives its shape to the body it inhabits. The final metaphor of the passage takes the form of an extended simile: "*just as* the Japanese . . . *so* in that moment. . . ." In examining Proust's use of this particular metaphor, the student might begin by considering the ways in which the metaphor is appropriate to the situation—that is, to both the eating of the cake dipped in tea and the ensuing recovery of the past. Beyond that he might consider how the Japanese paper metaphor is related to the soul metaphor, and how both of these are related to the theatrical simile ("like the scenery") which links them.

Finally, this consideration of metaphor should lead back to an awareness of tone. Though this passage is a translation from the original French, it captures the tone of the original with very high fidelity. How would you describe this tone? How should the passage sound if read aloud? What is the function of the repeated use of "and" in the last sentence (which is the last sentence in a whole section of the book)? How is the tone related to the metaphoric structure and the meaning of the passage? In sum, how do these two most important dimensions of the art of language—tone and metaphor—operate in this passage to control the response of a sensitive and careful reader? In getting at this question the student might try to paraphrase the passage without its metaphors and tonal qualities. Considering such a paraphrase, he might then ask to what extent the meaning *is* paraphrasable, and to what extent the meaning requires the images and rhythms of the passage itself.

the order of events is not likely to assume any special significance. But if the action is rearranged in time so that we encounter events out of their chronological sequence—through flashbacks or some other device— then the order should be given some attention. We must look for reasons behind this manipulation of chronology by the author. Why has he chosen to place this particular scene from the "past" next to this particular scene in the "present." Similarly, if we are following two actions in one story, now one and now the other, we should look for reasons why an incident from one sequence should be placed next to a particular incident in the other. Often we will find interesting parallels: similar situations that amount to a kind of repetition with variation. If character A gets into a situation and takes one kind of action while character B, in a similar situation takes a different action, we should be able to compare the two and contrast their distinctive behavior, thus learning more about both. This kind of comparison can also lead us quite properly to generalizations about the meaning of a work.

Significant kinds of repetition also occur in sections of a story which are not placed next to one another. This kind of repetition is an important element of design, and serves to tie separate parts of a story together, enriching and strengthening the whole structure. Structure in fiction is a very complicated notion, because it involves so many factors. We can think of structure in one sense as those elements which shape our experience as we move through the story. In this sense structure is close to plot. We can also think of structure as those elements which enable us to see a meaningful pattern in the whole work. In this sense structure is close to design. For if plot has to do with the dynamics or movement of fiction, design has to do with the statics of fiction—the way we see a whole story after we have stopped moving through it. When we become aware of design in reading, so that one part of a story reminds us of parts we have read earlier, we are actually involved in a movement counter to our progress through from beginning to end. Plot wants to move us along; design wants to delay our movement, to make us pause and "see." The counteraction of these two forces is one of the things which enriches our experience of fiction.

Design is often a matter of the repetition of images or metaphors. In considering the metaphors of drowning in *Mrs. Dalloway*, we have already begun an examination of the way metaphoric design can tie together quite different characters and situations. Now I should like to present a striking example of a rather different use of repetition in the design of a story. This is a case where two episodes in the life of the same character—separated by both pages of our reading and weeks in the life of the character—are brought together into powerful contrast by means of repetition with variation.

At the end of the second chapter of James Joyce's novel *A Portrait of the Artist as a Young Man*, the young man of the title, Stephen Dedalus, has been led by the urgings of physical desire into the arms of a prostitute. This is the last paragraph of that chapter:

> With a sudden movement she bowed his head and joined her lips to his and he read the meaning of her movements in her frank uplifted eyes. It was too much for him. He closed his eyes, surrendering himself to her, body and mind, conscious of nothing in the world but the dark pressure of her softly parting lips. They pressed upon his brain as upon his lips as though they were the vehicle of vague speech; and between them he felt an unknown and timid pressure, darker than the swoon of sin, softer than sound or odour.

By the end of the third chapter, Joyce has taken Stephen Dedalus through a period of disgust, remorse, and repentence. In the last paragraphs of the chapter we find Stephen receiving holy communion:

> He knelt before the altar with his classmates, holding the altar cloth with them over a living rail of hands. His hands were trembling, and his soul trembled as he heard the priest pass with the ciborium from communicant to communicant.
>
> —*Corpus Domini nostri.*
>
> Could it be? He knelt there sinless and timid: and he would hold upon his tongue the host and God would enter his purified body.

—*In vitam eternam. Amen.*

Another life! A life of grace and virtue and happiness! It was true.

—*Corpus Domini nostri.*

The ciborium had come to him.

In the last sentence of the second chapter, Stephen felt the woman's tongue, pressing through her kiss—"an unknown and timid pressure." In the last lines of the third chapter, his tongue receives the body of Our Lord. Could the contrast be made more striking, or more rich in emotional and intellectual implications? Design here is powerfully carrying out Joyce's intention, which is to make us see Stephen poised between sinful and holy extremes, both of which attract him powerfully, but neither of which can hold him finally —as the later chapters demonstrate. The focus on tongues in these two episodes is the crucial repeated element which makes the contrast Joyce wishes. And in the context of the whole story, it reminds us that tongues are not only for kissing or receiving the sacrament. They are also instruments of expression. Stephen ultimately must strive to express himself as an artist of languages, using his gift of tongues. In these two episodes, Stephen has been passive, the receiver. Later he will learn to speak out.

What we have been considering is the way that an object—in this case the tongue—can by its use in a fictional design acquire a metaphorical value that points in the direction of meaning. When this happens, the object becomes a symbol. The process of symbolism will be examined further in the commentary on "Clay" below.

PART TWO

THREE STORIES AND COMMENTARIES

INTRODUCTORY NOTE

These stories are intended to illustrate something of the range and variety of modern short fiction. The commentaries are attempts to illustrate ways in which the procedures outlined in the first part of this book may be employed in the reading of fiction. They may also be thought of as developments or refinements of those procedures. In writing them I have not sought to put the stories mechanically through every analytical process mentioned above, but rather have tried to fit the relevant and useful procedures to the appropriate aspects of each story. Some aspects of the discussions in the first part of this book, it should be remembered, are more directly aimed at long fiction than at such short pieces as are presented here. Others will be more relevant to one story than another. All this should serve as a reminder that *there is no method.*

MOONLIGHT
by Guy de Maupassant

His warlike name well suited the Abbé Marignan.*
He was a tall thin priest, full of zeal, his soul always
exalted but just. All his beliefs were fixed; they never
wavered. He sincerely believed that he understood his
God, entered into His plans, His wishes, His intentions.

As he strode down the aisle of his little country
church, sometimes a question would take shape in his
mind: "Now why has God done that?" He would seek
the answer stubbornly, putting himself in God's place,
and he nearly always found it. He was not one of those
who murmur with an air of pious humility, "O Lord,
your designs are impenetrable!" He would say to him-

* The Battle of Marignan (1515) was a great and bloody vic-
tory for Francis I and France.

Translated by R.S., with valuable advice and criticism from
Peter Clothier and the students in his U. of Iowa Translation
Workshop.

43

self: "I am the servant of God, I should know his purposes, and if I don't know them I should divine them."

Everything in nature seemed to him created with an absolute and admirable logic. The "why" and the "because" always balanced out. Dawns existed to make waking up a pleasure, days to ripen the crops, rain to water them, evening to prepare for slumber, and the night was dark for sleeping.

The four seasons were perfectly fitted to all the needs of agriculture; and it would never have occurred to the priest to suspect that nature has no intentions at all, and that, on the contrary, every living thing has bowed to the hard necessities of times, climates, and matter itself.

But he hated women, he hated them unconsciously and despised them by instinct. He often repeated the words of Christ: "Woman, what have I to do with thee?" and he added, "You'd think that not even God himself was happy with that particular piece of work." Woman for him was precisely that child twelve times unclean of whom the poet speaks. She was the temptress who had ensnared the first man and who still continued her damnable work—a weak creature, dangerous, curiously disturbing. And even more than her devilish body he hated her loving soul.

He had often felt the yearning affection of women, and, even though he knew himself invulnerable, he was exasperated by this need to love which always trembled in them.

God, in his opinion, had made woman only to tempt man and test him. Thus man should approach her with great care, ever fearful of traps. She was, in fact, even shaped like a trap, with her arms extended and her lips parted for a man.

He was indulgent only of nuns, made inoffensive by their vows; and he treated even them severely, because he felt stirring in the depths of their fettered hearts—those hearts so humbled—that eternal yearning which still sought him out, even though he was a priest.

He felt it in their gaze—more steeped in piety than that of monks—in their religious ecstasy tainted with sex, in their transports of love for Christ, which infuriated him because it was woman's love, fleshly love. He felt it—this wicked yearning—even in their docility, in the sweetness of their voices in talking to him, in their lowered eyes, and in their submissive tears when he rebuffed them rudely.

And he shook out his soutane on leaving the gates of a convent and strode quickly away as though fleeing from danger.

He had a niece who lived with her mother in a little house nearby. He was determined to make her a Sister of Charity.

She was pretty, light-headed, and impish. When the Abbé preached, she laughed; and when he got angry at her she kissed him eagerly, clasping him to her heart while he tried instinctively to escape this embrace which nevertheless gave him a taste of sweet happiness, waking deep within him those paternal impulses which slumber in every man.

Often he spoke to her of God—of his God—while walking beside her along country lanes. She scarcely listened but looked at the sky, the grass, the flowers, with a lively joy which showed in her eyes. Sometimes she leaped to catch some flying thing and brought it back to him, crying: "Look, uncle, how pretty it is. I want to pet it." And this impulse to "pet bugs" or nuzzle lilac blossoms disturbed, annoyed, sickened the priest, who discerned in it that ineradicable yearning which always springs up in the female heart.

Then, it happened that one day the sacristan's wife, who kept house for the Abbé Marignan, cautiously told him that his niece had a lover. The news shocked him terribly and he stopped, choking, with his face full of soap, for he was busy shaving.

When he recovered so that he could think and speak, he shouted: "It is not true, you are lying, Mélanie!"

But the good woman put her hand on her heart: "May the Good Lord strike me dead if I'm lying, M. le Curé. She goes out there every night I tell you, as soon as your sister's in bed. They meet down by the river. You've only to go and watch there between ten and midnight."

He stopped scraping his chin and started walking up and down violently, as he always did in his hours of solemn meditation. When he tried to finish shaving he cut himself three times between the nose and the ear.

All day he was silenced, swollen with indignation and rage. To his fury as a priest, confronted by love, the invincible, was added the exasperation of a strict father, of a guardian, of a confessor fooled, cheated, tricked by a child. He shared that self-centered feeling of suffocation experienced by parents whose daughter tells them she has—without them and despite them—chosen a husband.

After dinner he tried to read a bit, but he could not get into it. He got more and more exasperated. When ten o'clock struck he took down his walking stick, a formidable oaken cudgel he always used when making his evening rounds to visit the sick. And he smiled as he looked at this big club, whirling it about fiercely in his great countryman's fist. Then, suddenly, he raised it and, gritting his teeth, brought it down on a chair, knocking its splintered back to the floor.

He opened the door to go out, but stopped on the sill, surprised by a splendor of moonlight such as he had rarely seen.

And, endowed as he was with an exalted spirit—such as those poetical dreamers the Fathers of the Church might have had—he was immediately distracted, moved by the glorious and serene beauty of the pale night.

In his little garden, all bathed in soft light, the ordered ranks of his fruit trees traced on the path the shadows of their slender limbs, lightly veiled with foliage, while the giant honeysuckle, clinging to the wall of the house, exhaled a delicious, sugary breath that floated through the calm clear air like a ghostly perfume.

He began to breathe deeply, drinking the air as a drunkard drinks wine, and he took a few slow, dreaming, wondering steps, almost forgetting his niece.

When he reached the open country, he stopped to contemplate the fields all flooded with tender light, bathed in the delicate and languid charm that calm nights have. Incessantly the frogs gave out their short metallic note, and distant nightingales, inspiring dream not thought, blended their unstrung tune—a rapid throbbing music made for kisses—with the enchantment of the moonlight.

The Abbé pressed on, losing heart, though he could not tell why. He felt feeble, suddenly drained; he wanted to sit down, to stay there, to contemplate, to admire God in His handiwork.

Below, following the undulations of the little river, a tall line of poplars wound like a snake. A fine mist, a white vapor which the moonbeams pierced and turned to glowing silver, hung around and above the banks wrapping the whole tortuous watercourse in a sort of delicate and transparent gauze.

The priest halted again, struck to the depths of his soul by an irresistable wave of yearning.

And a doubt, a vague disturbance, came over him. He sensed within himself another of those questions he sometimes posed.

Why had God done this? Since the night is intended for sleep, for unconsciousness, for repose, for oblivion, why make it more charming than the day, sweeter than dawn or evening? And why this slow and seductive moon, which is more poetic than the sun and seems intended by its very delicacy to illumine things too fragile and mysterious for daylight, why should it come to make the shadows so transparent?

Why should the loveliest of songbirds not go to sleep with the others but linger on to sing in the disturbing shade?

Why this half-veil thrown over the world? Why this thrill in the heart, this stirring of the soul, this languor of the flesh?

Why this display of delights that men never see, since they are asleep in their beds? For whom was it intended, this sublime spectacle, this flood of poetry poured from the sky over the earth?

And the Abbé found no answer.

But then, down below, on the edge of the fields, under the vault of trees drenched with glowing mist, two shadows appeared, walking side by side.

The man was taller and held the neck of his lover and sometimes kissed her forehead. Their sudden appearance brought the still countryside to life, and it enfolded the young lovers like a setting divinely made for them. They seemed, the pair, a single being, the being for whom this calm and silent night was intended, and they moved toward the priest like a living answer, the answer to his question, flung back by his Master.

He stood still, his heart pounding in confusion, and he felt as if he were looking at a biblical scene, like the love of Ruth and Boaz, like the accomplishment of the will of God as presented in one of the great scenes of holy scripture. In his head echoed verses of the Song of Songs: the passionate cries, the calls of the flesh, all the ardent poetry of this poem that seethes with passionate yearning.

And he said to himself: "Perhaps God has made such nights to veil the loves of men with ideal beauty."

He recoiled before the couple who kept walking arm in arm. It was certainly his niece. But he asked himself now if he was not on the verge of disobeying God. Must not God permit love since he lavished upon it such visible splendor?

And he fled, distraught, almost ashamed, as if he had entered a temple where he had no right to be.

A COMMENTARY ON "MOONLIGHT"

This tale is essentially realistic. The events are ordinary, the geography recognizable; the characters can be assigned to a particular time, place, religion, and class. But the imposition of a pattern on this realistic material moves it in the direction of comic romance. It contains no detail presented for its own sake or as documentation of a way of life. Every piece of information given to us contributes to the comic pattern of the plot. We can see this if we consider the central character and what we know about him.

In this uncomplicated tale the Abbé Marignan is not only the central character, he is almost the only character. His niece and the housekeeper, Mélanie, exist only to the extent that they contribute to the Abbé's story. And the Abbé's story, if we consider its beginning and end, is a story of education, of a change in attitude. The change involves a dramatic shift in the priest's view of women and love. The story falls naturally into three sections of nearly equal length, of which the first is entirely devoted to the presentation of the Abbé's character. Even here a striking selectivity prevails. We learn about two facets of this character only: one is the nature of the priest's religious belief, presented in the first paragraph and elaborated in the next three; the other is the priest's attitude toward women and love, presented in the fourth paragraph and elaborated in the next five. These two attributes are absolutely vital to the story because his attitude toward love must be changed—this is what the story is "about"—and his religious belief is the lever by means of which the change is accomplished. All the information in the first four paragraphs prepares us for the priest's mental process as we follow it in the closing paragraphs of the story.

If we accept the justice of the priest's comic education, we accept with it a particular view of life. There is a touch of satire as well as comedy in this tale. The priest's view of the workings of the universe is being subjected to an ironic scrutiny which is implicit in the way the story is worked out, and is almost explicit in the point of view from which the story is told. Even the priest's name, Marignan, is touched with irony for those who recognize what it alludes to, since the victor of the Battle of Marignan, Francis I, was defeated and captured in his next campaign, as the Abbé is in *his* little struggle.

Exactly what is our perspective on the events of this little tale? We look into the mind of the Abbé but we do not see things from his point of view. The narrator has his own perspective which is revealed to us by the allusion to the Battle of Marignan and by other means. Consider the fourth paragraph:

> The four seasons were perfectly fitted to all the needs of agriculture; and it would never have occurred to the priest to suspect that nature has no intentions at all, and that, on the contrary, every living thing has bowed to the necessities of times, climates, and matter itself.

Up to the semi-colon, we are receiving a report on the priest's view—actually a continuation of the preceding paragraph. But after the semi-colon, we are being given another view of the world, one which "would never have occurred" to the Abbé himself. This other viewpoint—the narrator's—is in direct opposition to the priest's. Where the Abbé sees God's intentions everywhere, the narrator sees a nature without plan or purpose but still determining the quality of existence. There is a touch of naturalism in this view (a satiric hint of a chaotic, destructive world), which is counteracted by the purposeful pattern of the story itself. The narrator's views are closest to the surface in this paragraph, but once we are alert to them we can see them operating more subtly elsewhere. In the very first paragraph, for instance, the last two sentences are so emphatic in their repetition that they acquire a somewhat mocking tone. In them we learn not only that the priest's views are "fixed," but also that they "never wavered." We learn that the Abbé entered not only into God's "plans," but also into "his wishes, his intentions." This underlining of the rigidity and presumption of the priest's beliefs prepares us for his comeuppance and at the same time makes us unconsciously begin to wish for it.

Some of the metaphors used by the narrator also enrich the meaning of the work. The last sentence employs a simile which is appropriate and ironic. The priest flees from this love scene "as if he had entered into a temple where he had no right to be." The word "entered" (*pénétré*), of course, echoes ironically the penetration of the priest into God's designs, and is an interesting example of such designed repetition, but this penetration in the last sentence of the story is part of a metaphoric structure—a simile introduced by the expression "as if." The key word in the simile is "temple." The priest does not flee from a scene which outrages religion in order to take sanctuary in his church. In a comic reversal he flees from a scene which is itself religious, as he now understands it, and where he is the infidel profaning holy ground. This image of the temple, we should also note, has been prepared for by our first sight of the two lovers, under the "vault" of the trees.

Other metaphors operate with comparable subtlety. Consider the priest's first vision of this scene, as he pauses above it and looks at the winding river and the poplars lining its banks. The narrator, in describing the trees, says they "wound like a snake" (*serpentait*). He must have chosen this expression specifically to remind us of a similar idyllic love scene—the Garden of Eden —which also had its serpent. The suggestion is delicate and rich. The priest usually thinks of woman as "the temptress who had ensnared the first man," but in this scene nature itself and finally God seem to have conspired to surround this "sin" with beauty. And the Abbé enters a world in which he is as much an alien as the devil in paradise, though his intention is not to tempt but to prevent a fall.

Although this story is essenti lly a plot, it is not without design. The early sample of the Abbé's reasoning process is repeated at the end with its startling new conclusion that God "must permit love." And the temple simile in the last sentence reminds us of two related scenes: the Abbé striding so confidently down the aisle of his own church, and the Abbé leaving a convent of nuns with that same stride, after having shaken its contaminating dust of femininity off his soutane. He, who had been too pure to accept these nuns as his spiritual equals, is finally seen as profaning a temple of love. The design and the tone reinforce in various subtle ways the irony of the plot. The strength of this little story lies in the way all these elements cooperate to achieve its comic effect.

CLAY
by James Joyce

The matron had given her leave to go out as soon as the women's tea was over and Maria looked forward to her evening out. The kitchen was spick and span: the cook said you could see yourself in the big copper boilers. The fire was nice and bright and on one of the side-tables were four very big barmbracks. These barmbracks seemed uncut; but if you went closer you would see that they had been cut into long thick even slices and were ready to be handed round at tea. Maria had cut them herself.

Maria was a very, very small person indeed but she had a very long nose and a very long chin. She talked a little through her nose, always soothingly: *Yes, my dear*, and *No, my dear*. She was always sent for when the women quarrelled over their tubs and always succeeded in making peace. One day the matron had said to her:

—Maria, you are a veritable peace-maker!

And the sub-matron and two of the Board ladies had heard the compliment. And Ginger Mooney was always saying what she wouldn't do to the dummy who had charge of the irons if it wasn't for Maria. Everyone was so fond of Maria.

The women would have their tea at six o'clock and she would be able to get away before seven. From Ballsbridge to the Pillar, twenty minutes; from the Pillar to Drumcondra, twenty minutes; and twenty minutes to buy the things. She would be there before eight. She took out her purse with the silver clasps and read again the words *A Present from Belfast*. She was very fond of that purse because Joe had brought it to her five years before when he and Alphy had gone to Belfast on a Whit-Monday trip. In the purse were two half-crowns and some coppers. She would have five shillings clear after paying tram fare. What a nice evening they would have, all the children singing! Only she hoped that Joe wouldn't come in drunk. He was so different when he took any drink.

Often he had wanted her to go and live with them; but she would have felt herself in the way (though Joe's wife was ever so nice with her) and she had become accustomed to the life of the laundry. Joe was a good fellow. She had nursed him and Alphy too; and Joe used often say:

—Mamma is mamma but Maria is my proper mother.

After the break-up at home the boys had got her that position in the *Dublin by Lamplight* laundry, and she liked it. She used to have such a bad opinion of Protestants but now she thought they were very nice people, a little quiet and serious, but still very nice people to live with. Then she had her plants in the conservatory and she liked looking after them. She had lovely ferns and wax-plants and, whenever anyone came to visit her, she always gave the visitor one or two slips from her conservatory. There was one thing she didn't like and that was the tracts on the walls; but the matron was such a nice person to deal with, so genteel.

When the cook told her everything was ready she went into the women's room and began to pull the big bell. In a few minutes the women began to come in by twos and threes, wiping their steaming hands in their petticoats and pulling down the sleeves of their blouses over their red steaming arms. They settled down before their huge mugs which the cook and the dummy filled up with hot tea, already mixed with milk and sugar in huge tin cans. Maria superintended the distribution of the barmbrack and saw that every woman got her four slices. There was a great deal of laughing and joking during the meal. Lizzie Fleming said Maria was sure to get the ring and, though Fleming had said that for so many Hallow Eves, Maria had to laugh and say she didn't want any ring or man either; and when she laughed her grey-green eyes sparkled with disappointed shyness and the tip of her nose nearly met the tip of her chin. Then Ginger Mooney lifted up her mug of tea and proposed Maria's health while all the other women clattered with their mugs on the table, and said she was sorry she hadn't a sup of porter to drink it in. And Maria laughed again till the tip of her nose nearly met the tip of her chin and till her minute body nearly shook itself asunder because she knew that Mooney meant well though, of course, she had the notions of a common woman.

But wasn't Maria glad when the women had finished their tea and the cook and the dummy had begun to clear away the tea-things! She went into her little bed-room and, remembering that the next morning was a mass morning, changed the hand of the alarm from seven to six. Then she took off her working skirt and her house-boots and laid her best skirt out on the bed and her tiny dress-boots beside the foot of the bed. She changed her blouse too and, as she stood before the mirror, she thought of how she used to dress for mass on Sunday morning when she was a young girl; and she looked with quaint affection at the diminutive body which she had so often adorned. In spite of its years she found it a nice tidy little body.

When she got outside the streets were shining wtih rain and she was glad of her old brown raincloak. The

tram was full and she had to sit on the little stool at
the end of the car, facing all the people, with her toes
barely touching the floor. She arranged in her mind
all she was going to do and thought how much better
it was to be independent and to have your own money
in your pocket. She hoped they would have a nice
evening. She was sure they would but she could not
help thinking what a pity it was Alphy and Joe were
not speaking. They were always falling out now but
when they were boys together they used to be the
best of friends: but such was life.

She got out of her tram at the Pillar and ferreted
her way quickly among the crowds. She went into
Downes's cake-shop but the shop was so full of people
that it was a long time before she could get herself
attended to. She bought a dozen of mixed penny cakes,
and at last came out of the shop laden with a big bag.
Then she thought what else would she buy: she wanted
to buy something really nice. They would be sure to
have plenty of apples and nuts. It was hard to know
what to buy and all she could think of was cake. She
decided to buy some plumcake but Downes's plumcake had not enough almond icing on top of it so she
went over to a shop in Henry Street. Here she was a
long time in suiting herself and the stylish young lady
behind the counter, who was evidently a little annoyed
by her, asked her was it wedding-cake she wanted to
buy. That made Maria blush and smile at the young
lady; but the young lady took it all very seriously and

finally cut a thick slice of plumcake, parcelled it up and said:

—Two-and-four, please.

She thought she would have to stand in the Drumcondra tram because none of the young men seemed to notice her but an elderly gentleman made room for her. He was a stout gentleman and he wore a brown hard hat; he had a square red face and a greying moustache. Maria thought he was a colonel-looking gentleman and she reflected how much more polite he was than the young men who simply stared straight before them. The gentleman began to chat with her about Hallow Eve and the rainy weather. He supposed the bag was full of good things for the little ones and said it was only right that the youngsters should enjoy themselves while they were young. Maria agreed with him and favoured him with demure nods and hems. He was very nice with her, and when she was getting out at the Canal Bridge she thanked him and bowed, and he bowed to her and raised his hat and smiled agreeably; and while she was going up along the terrace, bending her tiny head under the rain, she thought how easy it was to know a gentleman even when he has a drop taken.

Everybody said: O, *here's Maria!* when she came to Joe's house. Joe was there, having come home from business, and all the children had their Sunday dresses on. There were two big girls in from next door and games were going on. Maria gave the bag of cakes to the eldest boy, Alphy, to divide and Mrs Donnelly said it was too good of her to bring such a big bag of cakes and made all the children say:

—Thanks, Maria.

But Maria said she had brought something special for papa and mamma, something they would be sure to like, and she began to look for her plumcake. She tried in Downes's bag and then in the pockets of her raincloak and then on the hallstand but nowhere could she find it. Then she asked all the children had any of them eaten it—by mistake, of course—but the children all said no and looked as if they did not like to eat cakes if they were to be accused of stealing. Everybody had a solution for the mystery and Mrs Donnelly said it was plain that Maria had left it behind her in the tram. Maria, remembering how confused the gentleman with the greyish moustache had made her, coloured with shame and vexation and disappointment. At the thought of the failure of her little surprise and of the two and fourpence she had thrown away for nothing she nearly cried outright.

But Joe said it didn't matter and made her sit down by the fire. He was very nice with her. He told her all that went on in his office, repeating for her a smart answer which he had made to the manager. Maria did not understand why Joe laughed so much over the answer he had made but she said that the manager must have been a very overbearing person to deal with. Joe said he wasn't so bad when you knew how to take him, that he was a decent sort so long as you didn't rub him the wrong way. Mrs Donnelly played the piano for the children and they danced and sang. Then the two next-door girls handed round the nuts. Nobody could find the nutcrackers and Joe was nearly getting cross over it and asked how did they expect Maria to crack nuts without a nutcracker. But Maria said she didn't like nuts and that they weren't to bother about her. Then Joe asked would she take a bottle of stout and Mrs Donnelly said there was port wine too in the house if she would prefer that. Maria said she would rather they didn't ask her to take anything: but Joe insisted.

So Maria let him have his way and they sat by the fire talking over old times and Maria thought she would put in a good word for Alphy. But Joe cried that God might strike him stone dead if ever he spoke a word to his brother again and Maria said she was sorry she had mentioned the matter. Mrs Donnelly told her husband it was a great shame for him to speak that way of his own flesh and blood but Joe said that Alphy was no brother of his and there was nearly being a row on the head of it. But Joe said he would not lose his temper on account of the night it was and asked his wife to open some more stout. The two next-door girls had arranged some Hallow Eve games and soon everything was merry again. Maria was delighted to see the children so merry and Joe and his wife in such good spirits. The next-door girls put some saucers on the table and then led the children up to the table, blindfold. One got the prayer-book and the other three got the water; and when one of the next-door girls got the ring Mrs Donnelly shook her finger at the blushing girl as much as to say: *O, I know all about it!* They insisted then on blindfolding Maria and leading her up to the table to see what she would get; and, while they were putting on the bandage, Maria laughed and laughed again till the top of her nose nearly met the tip of her chin.

They led her up to the table amid laughing and joking and she put her hand out in the air as she was told to do. She moved her hand about here and there in the air and descended on one of the saucers. She felt a soft wet substance with her fingers and was surprised that nobody spoke or took off her bandage. There was a pause for a few seconds; and then a great deal of scuffling and whispering. Somebody said something about the garden, and at last Mrs Donnelly said something very cross to one of the next-door girls and told her to throw it out at once: that was no play. Maria understood that it was wrong that time and so she had to do it over again: and this time she got the prayer-book.

After that Mrs Donnelly played Miss McCloud's Reel for the children and Joe made Maria take a glass of wine. Soon they were all quite merry again and Mrs Donnelly said Maria would enter a convent before the year was out because she had got the prayer-book.

Maria had never seen Joe so nice to her as he was that night, so full of pleasant talk and reminiscences. She said they were all very good to her.

At last the children grew tired and sleepy and Joe asked Maria would she not sing some little song before she went, one of the old songs. Mrs Donnelly said *Do, please, Maria!* and so Maria had to get up and stand beside the piano. Mrs Donnelly bade the children be quiet and listen to Maria's song. Then she played the prelude and said *Now, Maria!* and Maria, blushing very much, began to sing in a tiny quavering voice. She sang *I Dreamt that I Dwelt*, and when she came to the second verse she sang again:

> *I dreamt that I dwelt in marble halls*
> *With vassals and serfs at my side*
> *And of all who assembled within those walls*
> *That I was the hope and the pride.*
> *I had riches too great to count, could boast*
> *Of a high ancestral name,*
> *But I also dreamt, which pleased me most,*
> *That you loved me still the same.*

But no one tried to show her her mistake; and when she had ended her song Joe was very much moved. He said that there was no time like the long ago and no music for him like poor old Balfe, whatever other people might say; and his eyes filled up so much with tears that he could not find what he was looking for and in the end he had to ask his wife to tell him where the corkscrew was.

A COMMENTARY ON "CLAY"

I can remember vividly my first encounter with "Clay,"
and this is partly why I have chosen it for inclusion
here. I was a freshman in college and my roommate
handed me the anthology they were using in his English class and asked me what I made of one story in it
which baffled him. The story was "Clay," and I remember that it baffled me too. It was not like the stories
I knew and admired—by Poe, O. Henry, Maupassant.
It seemed to me to have no plot and to be about nothing in particular. By one of those ironies which operate
in life as well as in art, I have since devoted a good
deal of my time to working on Joyce. So "Clay" is
here both because I know it well and respect it and
because I can remember so well what it was like not to
understand it.

Like "Moonlight" it is realistic, dealing with ordinary people and situations. It is, in fact, much more
concerned to document a kind of reality than to tell a
crisp and comic tale. It is more realistic than "Moonlight" and more pathetic than comic in its effect. As
the Abbé Marignan's story is amusing, Maria's is
sad. And as his story is one of education, hers is
one of revelation. He *learns* from his experience; she
is revealed to us through her experience, but without
any increase in awareness on her part. The Abbé's day,
after all, is an extraordinary one in his life. Maria's is

merely typical. Nothing of great importance happens in it. This is one reason why "Clay" can be so baffling. It is hard to "see" a story in it, since nothing of any consequence happens. Nevertheless, it is a story, and it will respond to a careful consideration of its elements.

To begin with the matter of plot, it is not easy to find one in "Clay," but one is there all the same. Part of it has to do with the Halloween game that Maria and the others play. The game is not explained but there are enough clues in the story for us to reconstruct its method. We first hear of the game while Maria is still at the laundry:

> There was a great deal of laughing and joking during the meal. Lizzie Fleming said Maria was sure to get the ring and, though Fleming had said that for so many Hallow Eves, Maria had to laugh and say she didn't want any ring or any man either; and when she laughed her grey-green eyes sparkled with disappointed shyness and the tip of her nose nearly met the tip of her chin.

Later, Maria plays the game at her brother's house, so that, taken together, the two scenes make the beginning and end of a line of action in the story. And, since the title points directly toward the second of these scenes, we are surely right to consider it important. In this scene we first learn more about the operation of the game, as the children and the next-door girls play it:

The next-door girls put some saucers on the table
and then led the children up to the table, blindfold. One got the prayer-book and the other three
got the water; and when one of the next-door
girls got the ring Mrs Donnelly shook her finger
at the blushing girl as much as to say: *O, I know
all about it!*

And later, after the game has gone "wrong" once and
been played over, Maria is gently teased by Mrs Donnelly also:

. . . Mrs Donnelly said Maria would enter a convent before the year was out because she had got
the prayer-book.

The game, as we can reconstruct it from the clues in
these three passages, is a simple, fortune-telling affair.
A blind-folded person chooses among three saucers
and the choice indicates the future event. The ring
indicates marriage, the prayer-book foretells entering
the Church, and the water—we are not told, but I
should guess a sea-voyage. In reading this story we
must continue to perform exactly this kind of recon-
struction. Where Maupassant told us everything he
wanted us to know in the most direct way possible,
Joyce is *in*direct, making us do a good deal of interpretive labor ourselves. But having figured out the
game, we must now arrive at an understanding of its
significance in Maria's story.

At the beginning of this line of action, Maria was

teased by Lizzie Fleming about being "sure to get the ring"—which would mean marriage. At the end she is teased about having got the prayer-book, which means a life of chaste seclusion from the world. But between these moments, Maria has actually made her real selection:

> They led her up to the table amid laughing and joking and she put out her hand out in the air as she was told to do. She moved her hand about here and there in the air and descended on one of the saucers. She felt a soft wet substance with her fingers and was surprised that nobody spoke or took off her bandage. There was a pause for a few seconds; and then a great deal of scuffling and whispering. Somebody said something about the garden, and at last Mrs Donnelly said something very cross to one of the next-door girls and told her to throw it out at once: that was no play. Maria understood that it was wrong that time and so she had to do it over again: and this time she got the prayer-book.

By calling his story "Clay," Joyce made sure that we would be able to understand this episode and its significance, even though Maria herself, from whose point of view we are perceiving things, never realizes what substance she has encountered. The next-door girls have played a trick on her by putting clay into one of the saucers. We know what the ring, prayer-book, and water signify in this game. But clay is not regularly a part of it. Its significance is a matter for our interpretation. Clearly, we will not be far wrong if we associate it with death, realizing that Maria is not likely to marry or enter a convent, but certainly is destined to die and become clay—as are we all. Clay is the substance out of which the first man was made. It conveys the essence of human frailty. Indeed, "that was no play." The clay intrudes on this Halloween scene like a ghostly presence, reminding us of the reality of death and decomposition. Thus, with some scrutiny, this strand of the action becomes both clear and meaningful. But at least one other must be accounted for. If we are to grasp the entire story we must understand such episodes as Maria admiring her body in the mirror, Maria responding to the "colonel-looking gentlemen," Maria losing her plumcake, and Maria mistaking the verses of her song.

Since the mistake in singing is the very last thing in "Clay," we might well consider it for possible revelations. What mistake does Maria make? "When she came to the second verse she sang again: . . . . But no one tried to show her her mistake." She repeats the first verse, which is to say, she leaves out the second. What does she leave out? The omitted second verse goes this way:

> *I dreamt that suitors sought my hand,*
> *That knights on bended knee,*
> *And with vows no maiden heart could withstand,*
> *They pledged their faith to me.*

> *And I dreamt that one of that noble band,*
> *Came forth my heart to claim,*
> *But I also dreamt, which charmed me most,*
> *That you loved me all the same.*

Joyce could have told us what was in this verse that Maria omitted, but he chose simply to leave out what she left out and include the verse she repeated. He made sure we knew she had left something out, but he did not tell us its nature. As with the game, he insists that we do the work of interpretation, which in this case includes research into "I Dreamt that I Dwelt," so that we can supply the missing verse. He continually requires us to share the work of constructing this story in order to understand it. But what does the missing verse tell us? It tell us that Maria unconsciously rebelled at singing "suitors sought my hand"; that a subject such as "vows that no maiden heart could withstand" bothered her enough that she repressed it and "forgot" the second verse. Can we relate this to the other episodes in the story?

When Lizzie Fleming teased her and predicted she would "get the ring," Maria "had to laugh and say she didn't want any ring or man either." But she adorns her "nice tidy little body," and she gets so flustered by an inebriated "colonel-looking gentleman" that she misplaces her plumcake while talking to him. In its very different way from Maupassant's, Joyce story is also about feminine *"tendresse,"* or *"yearning."* The missing verse fits into this pattern perfectly. Maria is a reluctant spinster, homely as a Halloween witch, with the tip of her nose nearly meeting the tip of her chin. She feels superior to the "common" women who work in the *Dublin by Lamplight* laundry (a title intended to suggest that the laundresses have been reclaimed from a distinctly "fallen" status), but she takes several drinks when Joe "makes" her. Her appetites are more like those of the "common" women than she would admit. All in all, she is a pathetic figure—a "peacemaker" whose "children" have quarreled so bitterly that she is powerless to reconcile them, and whose suspicions about the children eating her missing plumcake turn them temporarily against her and perhaps lead to the trick by the next-door girls. Clay certainly, common clay.

The title of this story points much more insistently toward its meaning than does the title of "Moonlight" (though the French title, "Clair de Lune," is stronger than its English equivalent in suggesting a metaphoric "light" in the sense of mental illumination). Like the title of "Moonlight," the title of "Clay" points toward something that is present in the story, but this clay of Joyce's story is more richly and subtly meaningful than Maupassant's moonlight. The substance, clay, acquires metaphorical suggestions of mortality and common human weakness. The object in the story—that dish of clay in the Halloween game—becomes a symbol for these complicated qualities. And symbolism is the richest and most complicated of metaphorical processes.

Metaphorical possibilities range from the simple and straightforward simile to the symbol. The simile indicates precisely the nature of the comparison it makes with words like "as" and "so." But the symbol opens out from an object or image in the direction of an unspecified meaning. We should add that though the meaning of a symbol is extensive and not precisely limited, this meaning is always directed and controlled in some way. A symbol in a work of fiction, like the clay in this story, cannot be made to "mean" anything we happen to associate with the word "clay." Only those associations both suggested by the substance clay and actually related to Maria's fictional situation belong in our interpretation of the story. Meanings like "mortality" and "common weakness" are traditionally associated with clay in Western tradition, from the Bible on, and clay is used to symbolize similar things in other cultures as well. But we must demonstrate a connection between these traditional meanings and the story in order to establish their appropriateness. Plot, character, and symbol work together to shape our final understanding of the story.

We should note in passing that "Clay" is a special kind of short story in that it is actually part of a sequence of stories put together by its author for a purpose beyond that realizable in any single short piece. In this case, Joyce called his sequence *Dubliners* and meant it as a representation of life in his native city of Dublin. In its proper setting, the meaning of

"Clay" chimes with the meaning of the other stories, as Maria's spinsterhood and common humanity are echoed by and contrasted with the situations and qualities of other Dubliners. But even though it gains in resonance when placed in *Dubliners*, "Clay" is quite sufficient to be of interest by itself.

Aside from its central symbol, Joyce is sparing of metaphor in "Clay." But he is very careful about his control of tone. The tone he establishes at the beginning never falters. How should it be described? "The kitchen was spick and span. . . . The fire was nice and bright." What kind of prose is this? Or consider the short fourth paragraph:

> And the sub-matron and two of the Board ladies had heard the compliment. And Ginger Mooney was always saying what she wouldn't do to the dummy who had charge of the irons if it wasn't for Maria. Everyone was so fond of Maria.

The syntactical pattern of "And . . . and . . . . And" is just one facet of the excessive simplicity of this prose. It is echoed by the quality of cliché that we find in phrases like "spick and span" or "nice and bright." Though Maria herself is not telling this story to us, the narrator is using language closely approaching her own. That is one reason why any striking use of metaphor has been ruled out. Complicated sentences, complex words, and brilliant turns of phrase are all inappropriate here. Joyce said once that he had written

Dubliners in a style of "scrupulous meanness." That expression is exactly appropriate to the style of "Clay." In the paragraph we are considering, this linguistic situation is actually somewhat like the one in the first paragraph that was quoted from *Mrs. Dalloway* in the section on point of view, above (see p. 28): simple, even banal language; and a "so" in the last sentence. Is the tone of the two paragraphs—or of the two "so's"—exactly the same? I think not. The excessive simplicity of Virginia Woolf's prose at this point is entirely devoted to mockery of Sir William Bradshaw. But Joyce's simplicity is in considerable part devoted to giving us Maria's own view of her situation. Her view is undoubtedly limited. Everyone is not *so* fond of her as she would like to think. But we are not really standing off from her and subjecting her to an ironic scrutiny. We are *with* her to some extent here, as well as detached from her. The paragraph in *Mrs. Dalloway* is almost pure satire. The paragraph in "Clay" is pathos mainly, with perhaps a slight admixture of satire.

All the way through the story, Joyce keeps very close not only to a style of language appropriate to Maria, but also to Maria's perspective. Only rarely, as when Maria responds to Lizzie's teasing, does he tell us directly something she could not perceive herself. And there, when he tells us her "eyes sparkled with disappointed shyness," he is giving us an important clue to the "disappointed" quality of her spinsterhood. Usually he avoids such direct transcendence of Maria's perspective and makes us do the work of inference ourselves. Even at the end, when he tells us something that Maria does not know—that she has left out a verse of the song—he does not tell us what is in the verse, for to do so would take us too far from her perspective. By holding us so close to the viewpoint of his central character, Joyce makes it necessary for us to infer a good deal in order to achieve a distance from her sufficient to focus on her with the clarity of detachment. In effect, he makes us see Maria with a double vision, engaged and detached, sympathetic and ironic. And not only Maria but the other characters as well must be seen in this way. Joe, at the close of the story, weeping so much he cannot find the corkscrew to open another bottle, could be seen as a caricature only—another drunken, sentimental, stage Irishman. But Joe's booze-induced sentimentality is also genuine warmth—a mixture of the genuine and the spurious which is, for better or worse, very common in life. Joyce leaves the evaluation to us. The comic clarity of Maupassant does make, in a sense, a better story. The delicacy and complexity of Joyce make a more realistic one. Fortunately, we do not have to choose between one and the other. We can have both ways, and many more, whenever we went.

Design in "Clay" is mainly a matter of the organization of parts to bear on the revelation of Maria's common disappointments. The central symbol of the clay itself, which is established in the story's climactic episode, is the pivot around which everything else turns. The story appears to us to be almost a plotless, designless "slice of life," and we have to look carefully to note the care of its construction. Actually, design operates much more powerfully in *Dubliners* as a whole than in any single story. The arrangement of stories was very carefully worked out by Joyce to achieve certain juxtapositions, and the stories are designed so that each contains elements that repeat and echo their counterparts in the others. The larger any work is, the more important plot and design become as elements of coherence. A collection of stories, which has no plot, must depend extensively on design for its structural interconnections. But Joyce preferred design to plot, and his longest narratives, *Ulysses* and *Finnegans Wake*, are scantily plotted and elaborately designed.

THEME OF THE TRAITOR
AND THE HERO
by J. L. Borges

So the Platonic year
Whirls out new right and wrong,
Whirls in the old instead;
All men are dancers and their tread
Goes to the barbarous clangour of a gong.
                    W. B. Yeats: *The Tower*

Under the notable influence of Chesterton (contriver
and embellisher of elegant mysteries) and the palace
counselor Leibniz (inventor of the pre-established harmony), in my idle afternoons I have imagined this story
plot which I shall perhaps write some-day and which
already justifies me somehow. Details, rectifications,
adjustments are lacking; there are zones of the story
not yet revealed to me; today, January 3rd, 1944, I
seem to see it as follows:

The action takes place in an oppressed and tenacious country: Poland, Ireland, the Venetian Republic, some South American or Balkan state . . . Or rather it has taken place, since, though the narrator is contemporary, his story occurred towards the middle or the beginning of the nineteenth century. Let us say (for narrative convenience) Ireland; let us say in 1824. The narrator's name is Ryan; he is the great-grandson of the young, the heroic, the beautiful, the assassinated Fergus Kilpatrick, whose grave was mysteriously violated, whose name illustrated the verses of Browning and Hugo, whose statue presides over a gray hill amid red marshes.

Kilpatrick was a conspirator, a secret and glorious captain of conspirators; like Moses, who from the land of Moab glimpsed but could not reach the promised land, Kilpatrick perished on the eve of the victorious revolt which he had premeditated and dreamt of. The first centenary of his death draws near; the circumstances of the crime are enigmatic; Ryan, engaged in writing a biography of the hero, discovers that the enigma exceeds the confines of a simple police investigation. Kilpatrick was murdered in a theater; the British police never found the killer; the historians maintain that this scarcely soils their good reputation, since it was probably the police themselves who had him killed. Other facets of the enigma disturb Ryan. They are of a cyclic nature: they seem to repeat or combine events of remote regions, or remote ages. For example, no one is unaware that the officers who examined the hero's body found a sealed letter in which he was warned of the risk of attending the theater that evening; likewise Julius Caesar, on his way to the place where his friends' daggers awaited him, received a note he never read, in which the treachery was declared along with the traitors' names. Caesar's wife, Calpurnia, saw in a dream the destruction of a tower decreed him by the Senate; false and anonymous rumors on the eve of Kilpatrick's death publicized throughout the country that the circular tower of Kilgarvan had burned, which could be taken as a presage, for he had been born in Kilgarvan. These parallelisms (and others) between the story of Caesar and the story of an Irish conspirator lead Ryan to suppose the existence of a secret form of time, a pattern of repeated lines. He thinks of the decimal history conceived by Condorcet, of the morphologies proposed by Hegel, Spengler and Vico, of Hesiod's men, who degenerate from gold to iron. He thinks of the transmigration of souls, a doctrine that lends horror to Celtic literature and that Caesar himself attributed to the British druids; he thinks that, before having been Fergus Kilpatrick, Fergus Kilpatrick was Julius Caesar. He is rescued from these circular labyrinths by a curious finding, a finding which then sinks him into other, more inextricable and heterogeneous labyrinths: certain words uttered by a beggar who spoke with Fergus Kilpatrick the day of his death were prefigured by

Shakespeare in the tragedy *Macbeth*. That history should have copied history was already sufficiently astonishing; that history should copy literature was inconceivable . . . Ryan finds that, in 1814, James Alexander Nolan, the oldest of the hero's companions, had translated the principal dramas of Shakespeare into Gaelic; among these was *Julius Caesar*. He also discovers in the archives the manuscript of an article by Nolan on the Swiss *Festspiele:* vast and errant theatrical representations which require thousands of actors and repeat historical episodes in the very cities and mountains where they took place. Another unpublished document reveals to him that, a few days before the end, Kilpatrick, presiding over the last meeting, had signed the order for the execution of a traitor whose name had been deleted from the records. This order does not accord with Kilpatrick's merciful nature. Ryan investigates the matter (this investigation is one of the gaps in my plot) and manages to decipher the enigma.

Kilpatrick was killed in a theater, but the entire city was a theater as well, and the actors were legion, and the drama crowned by his death extended over many days and many nights. This is what happened:

On the 2nd of August, 1824, the conspirators gathered. The country was ripe for revolt; something, however, always failed: there was a traitor in the group. Fergus Kilpatrick had charged James Nolan with the responsibility of discovering the traitor. Nolan carried out his assignment: he announced in the very midst of the meeting that the traitor was Kilpatrick himself. He demonstrated the truth of his accusations with irrefutable proof; the conspirators condemned their president to die. He signed his own sentence, but begged that his punishment not harm his country.

It was then that Nolan conceived his strange scheme. Ireland idolized Kilpatrick; the most tenuous suspicion of his infamy would have jeopardized the revolt; Nolan proposed a plan which made of the traitor's execution an instrument for the country's emancipation. He suggested that the condemned man die at the hands of an unknown assassin in deliberately dramatic circumstances which would remain engraved in the imagination of the people and would hasten the revolt. Kilpatrick swore he would take part in the scheme, which gave him the occasion to redeem himself and for which his death would provide the final flourish.

Nolan, urged on by time, was not able to invent all the circumstances of the multiple execution; he had to plagiarize another dramatist, the English enemy William Shakespeare. He repeated scenes from *Macbeth*, from *Julius Caesar*. The public and secret enactment comprised various days. The condemned man entered Dublin, discussed, acted, prayed, reproved, uttered words of pathos, and each of these gestures, to be reflected in his glory, had been pre-established by Nolan. Hundreds of actors collaborated with the protagonist; the role of some was complex; that of others momentary. The things they did and said endure in the history books, in the impassioned memory of Ireland. Kilpatrick, swept along by this minutely detailed destiny which both redeemed him and destroyed him, more than once enriched the text of his judge with improvised acts and words. Thus the populous drama unfolded in time, until on the 6th of August, 1824, in a theater box with funereal curtains prefiguring Lincoln's, a long-desired bullet entered the breast of the traitor and hero, who, amid two effusions of sudden blood, was scarcely able to articulate a few foreseen words.

In Nolan's work, the passages imitated from Shakespeare are the *least* dramatic; Ryan suspects that the author interpolated them so that in the future someone might hit upon the truth. He understands that he too forms part of Nolan's plot . . . After a series of tenacious hesitations, he resolves to keep his discovery silent. He publishes a book dedicated to the hero's glory; this too, perhaps, was foreseen.

A COMMENTARY ON "THE THEME OF THE
TRAITOR AND THE HERO"

The first paragraph of Borges's story indicates unmistakably how far removed it is from the realism of Maupassant and Joyce. Instead of presenting us with a character situated in a world, it presents us with an

idea for a "story plot which I shall perhaps write some-
day." This story does not pretend to be a slice of life.
It does not even pretend to be a finished story: "Details, rectifications, adjustments are lacking; there are
zones of the story not yet revealed to me." It is hard
to see how fiction could insist more resolutely on its
fictional character. Moreover, despite its shortness, the
story consists of a number of separate plots or lines
of action. The narrator himself, whom we might call
Borges (italicized to distinguish him from the author,
Borges), is telling us about Ryan, a man who is trying
to write a biography. Ryan, himself a narrator, is trying to write the life of his ancestor Fergus Kilpatrick.
In particular, Ryan is trying to account for the mysterious manner of Kilpatrick's death in a theater. In
the first sentence *Borges* tells us he has "imagined"
this story under the influence of two other writers:
Chesterton, the author of certain detective-mysteries,
and Leibniz (or Leibnitz), a politician-mathematician-
historian-philosopher who developed a theory in which
the world is seen as an arrangement of harmoniously
related substances. By notifying us that a mystery
writer and a philosopher have inspired this tale, *Borges*
suggests that we should be alert for clues and ideas.
The story offers us a mystery about the death of
Fergus Kilpatrick, complete with clues and solution;
and the solution suggests a certain view of the world,
a philosophical position.

Along with Ryan, the detective-biographer, we follow the clues about the murder of Fergus Kilpatrick. We discover not only that James Nolan was responsible for his death, but that Nolan also stage-managed all the events which surrounded that death: "Kilpatrick was killed in a theater, but the entire city was a theater as well." Nolan, who was an expert on the Swiss *Festspiele*, had arranged a gigantic play. But this one, with its cast of thousands, was not a re-enactment of history in the form of fiction. It was fiction becoming history: "The things they did and said endure in the history books." The whole episode, which also prefigured the actual death of Lincoln, is referred to as Nolan's "work"—which it is, since he created it. *Borges*'s story closes with this paragraph:

> In Nolan's work, the passages imitated from Shakespeare are the *least* dramatic; Ryan suspects that the author interpolated them so that in the future someone might hit upon the truth. He understands that he too forms part of Nolan's plot . . . After a series of tenacious hesitations, he resolves to keep his discovery silent. He publishes a book dedicated to the hero's glory; this too, perhaps, was foreseen.

Ryan, the historian, has set out to discover historical truth about certain characters who lived in the past. He will then put them in a history book. What he discovers, however, is that he himself is perhaps a character in a fictional work designed by James Nolan; and his part is not that of truthful historian but of deceitful falsifier of history. He accepts the role as Kilpatrick accepted his, and plays the assigned part. But of course this part was really assigned by *Borges*, who tells us that he has made the whole thing up "in my idle afternoons." And behind this fictional *Borges* there stands another Borges who has made up this one, idle afternoons and all. And perhaps behind that one. . . .

We end, finally, as characters in someone's great design ourselves, as we sit reading Borges's pages, wondering whether the world is really organized according to a "pre-established harmony" or not. The quotation from Yeats, which is set before the story as its epigraph, proposes a cyclical theory of history. It is taken from a poem, "Nineteen Hundred and Nineteen," written by the poet during the Irish "Troubles," which began with an uprising, like many others plotted in Ireland, but ended in success—only to be followed by civil war. The poem, which Yeats included in his volume *The Tower*, is appropriate to the story in a very immediate way. But its main purpose is to add its voice to the cyclical theory of history that Borges is proposing in his story. The story is not a logical argument for this view. It merely asks "What if . . . ?". If history moves in cycles according to a pre-established harmony, then the sort of thing presented here might well occur. Questions like, "Does this sort of thing actually occur?" are left open to our thought. But Borges directs our thought along these lines. Instead of simply moving continually from old to new, history may—as Yeats suggests—whirl out the new and whirl in the old. It may move not in a line but in a circle or spiral. Borges's story can be seen as a variation on this theme in the philosophy of history.

Thus, in his tale Borges displays no special interest in the psychology of his characters or in the specific sociology of their environment. His Ireland is not Joyce's. Nor is it Yeats's. It is not even necessarily Ireland. It could be Poland or "some South American or Balkan state," as long as it is "oppressed and tenacious." The crowded plot and elaborate design of this little story overwhelm the characters. Idea and pattern, and the idea *of* pattern, dominate our vision. Borges has moved far from realism in telling us the stories of Ryan, Kilpatrick, and Nolan. Their tragi-comic histories exist for us mainly as a way of encouraging a pleasurable speculation—what Poe called "ratiocination." Philosophy can be seen as a serious playing with ideas. Borges embraces this playfulness and makes philosophy into fiction.

The title of this fable also encourages us to take a detached and speculative view of its "theme." What are traitors and heroes, it asks? One answer proposed is that traitors and heroes are people whom the history books present as traitors and heroes. Kilpatrick, of course, could be seen as either or both: his death being the execution of a traitor and the martyrdom of a hero who redeems himself by playing a role. Which is the "real" Kilpatrick? And is James Alexander Nolan, the stage-manager and executioner, a hero or traitor? And Ryan, who falsifies history for the sake of an ideal?

Whereas Joyce took a day in the life of an insignificant person and presented it with great care and seriousness, Borges takes the ideas of philosophers of history (like those he mentions: Condorcet, Hegel, Spengler, and Vico) and plays a fictional game with them. The possibilities of fiction are as various as man himself, and are continually renewed and refreshed by writers who offer us new perspectives on the universe. What every writer of fiction proposes to us is his own view of the world. He may look at it with a microscope or an inverted telescope. His lenses may be clear or colored. He may seek a photographic verisimilitude or offer us idealization or caricature. But every genuine writer of fiction offers us refined perception or expanded vision. It is because fiction enlarges and enhances our dealings with reality that we cherish it so highly.